AHHHHH!!! I Can't Take This Anymore!

My Journey Through Perimenopause

The Royal Candlelight Presents

AHHHH!!!

I Can't Take This Anymore!

My Journey Through Perimenopause

by

Cynthia Jennings

Royal Candlelight Christian Publishing Company

"Royalty in the Making"

AHHH!!! I Can't Take This Anymore
© 2018 by Royal Candlelight Christian Publishing Company
ISBN: 13-9780999284513

Published by: Royal Candlelight Christian Publishing Company
www.royalcandlelight.com
info@royalcandlelight.com

Email Address: royal.candlelight@hotmail.com
Internet TV Station Website: Ustreamtv.com *(Royal Candlelight)*
Editorial Team: Rachel Starr Thomson & Mercy Hope
Graphic & Media Arts Designer: Talon Williams
Book Interior Layout Designer: Lynn Williams
Sales & Marketing Director: Paul Williams
Social Media Strategist Team

Scripture quotations marked NASB was taken from The Hebrew-Greek Key Word Study Bible, New American Standard Bible, Revised Edition © 1984, 1990, 2008 by AMG International, Inc. These Scripture quotations marked NASB are from the *New American Standard Bible,* © 1960, 1962, 1963, 1968, 1971, 1972, 1973, 1975, 1977 by The Lockman Foundation. Used by permission. Scripture quotations marked "KJV" are from the King James Version of the Bible. Public domain.

ALL RIGHTS RESERVED
No portion of this publication may be reproduced, stored in a retrieval system, or transmitted in any form or by any means—electronic, mechanical, photocopy, recording or any other except for brief quotations in printed reviews or articles, without the prior permission of the publisher.

Printed in the United States of America

Contents

Acknowledgements	To God, My Husband and My Children	5
Dedications	To All Women	6
Foreword	By Anita Morris, Ed. D.	8
Introduction	God's Grace Is Sufficient!	10
The Facts	What Is Perimenopause?	12
My Journey	The Unexpected Season	14
Chapter 1	Crying Spell	21
Chapter 2	Fatigue, Sleepiness, and Exhaustion	26
Chapter 3	Anger and Rage	31
Chapter 4	Nausea and Queasiness	36
Chapter 5	Headaches and Migraines	41
Chapter 6	Night Sweats, Hot Flashes and Freezing Cold	47
Chapter 7	Stress Incontinence	52
Chapter 8	Bloating and Weight Gain	57
Chapter 9	Joint Pains and Boobs On Fire	64
Chapter 10	Digestive Issues	71
Chapter 11	Decreased Motor Coordination and Clumsiness	76
Chapter 12	Increased Hair Loss and Thinning (CCCA)	81
Chapter 13	My Husband's Perspective of My Journey	89
Articles	Cynthia Jennings "Pearls of Wisdom"	102
Author	Cynthia Jennings Biography	110
RCCPC	Advertisements to Christian Authors	114

Acknowledgements
To
God, The Father, The Son & The Holy Spirit
My Husband and My Children

I would like to first thank Father God and His Son Jesus Christ through the leading and guiding of The Holy Spirit for giving me the vision to pen this book.

To my husband Tracy, our son Reggie and our daughter Traci Nicole. Where do I begin? I know some days it seemed difficult to decipher how to deal with me but each of you, in your own special way, made sure that I did not feel any of the discomfort or confusion you may have been feeling. I thank you for your patience and understanding but most importantly, I thank you for your prayers.

When I told all of you I wanted to write a book about my journey through perimenopause I received nothing but encouragement especially on those days when I doubted myself. Words cannot express the gratitude I have for your love and support and for believing in me.

Dedications

To all the women who think they are traveling this journey alone I'm here as a witness to let you know you are not alone, but I sincerely know and understand how you are feeling. At the onset of my journey I too truly believed I was all alone and no one else would or could possibly understand what I was experiencing.

Albeit the journey will have some days where you feel completely hopeless and alone, but the best part of the journey is when you realize you are not alone. When I say you are not alone I am not talking about your physical support system. I am talking about the support and comfort that you will receive that no other person can match, and that is the comfort of knowing that Father God through His Son Jesus Christ will always be there with you.

Even on the worst days of my journey I learned to turn and trust God's Word without questions and I learned to not only listen to The Holy Spirit but be obedient to what The Holy Spirit was telling me. Had I waddled in my perimenopausal pity party the very words you are reading would not have happened. You see while in the midst of one of my most horrific moments of my journey I clearly and distinctly heard The Holy Spirit say, "what you are going through is not for you, get out of your pity party so you can help someone else who does not have anyone to turn to nor know the direction in which to turn." My goal is to be of support and encouragement to any woman who feels they are traveling this perimenopausal journey alone.

FOREWORD

AHHHH!!! I CAN'T TAKE THIS ANYMORE is an enlightening, inspirational quick-read. Inside the covers, you will find bible scriptures, facts, opinions, personal anecdotes, and clinical-based information about perimenopause, more commonly known as premenopause. Premenopause is a very REAL condition rarely discussed in everyday conversations and is a topic many women still consider taboo.

Cynthia Jennings, my neighbor, and friend, is very transparent throughout this book on the subject. She describes her personal, premenopausal symptoms ranging from barely noticeable to full-blown "episodes." Jennings describes how she revealed these experiences to her husband, children, small group and ministry. She also includes spiritual, emotional, and medical remedies in this text to express the various ways this condition may be treated. Throughout these chapters Jennings makes it abundantly clear there is no "one-way fits all" remedy for premenopause.

Many people experience or know others who are affected by premenopausal issues. Cynthia's husband,

Pastor Tracy Jennings, describes in this book his personal reflections on her perimenopausal episodes. Pastor Jennings recounts some of his thoughts, feelings, and how he ultimately provided his wife assistance in a God-fearing and loving manner.

At the end of each chapter, readers have the opportunity to self-reflect and journal on the note pages about this season in their life. The support delivered in this book is extremely encouraging to woman in this walk of life, and helps them understand they are not traveling this journey alone.

Thank you, Cynthia, for the loyal friendship you continually extend to me and my family. Most of all, thank you on behalf of the countless readers for being obedient and boldly exposing us to your calling from the Holy Spirit, when he told you: *"What you are going through is not for you, get out of your pity party so you can help someone who does not have anyone to turn to, or know the direction in which to turn."*

Anita Morris, Ed. D.

INTRODUCTION

God's Grace Is Sufficient!

"Let us then approach God's throne of grace with confidence, so that we may receive mercy and find grace to help us in our time of need." —Hebrews 4:16 (NIV)

"But he said to me, "My grace is sufficient for you, for my power is made perfect in weakness." Therefore I will boast all the more gladly of my weaknesses, so that the power of Christ may rest upon me." —2 Corinthians 12:9 (NIV)

I don't know exactly when I started into perimenopause but around February 2013, *at age 45,* I began to have weird symptoms. I did some research and I realized the majority of the symptoms I was experiencing were due to perimenopause. I was initially apprehensive to discuss it with my husband for several reasons. I felt as if he would not understand what I was going through and that he would think it was all in my head.

Honestly, I didn't even fully understand, so how could I explain it to him? I didn't know how he would react. What a relief that when I did open up to him about it he was very supportive. I believe he did a little research on his own to educate himself on perimenopause and because of that he has been a great support when I experience what he lovingly calls "episodes."

    I had a conversation with my children the summer of 2013 to explain it to them and they too were very receptive and supportive.

FACTS ON PERIMENOPAUSE

What is perimenopause? Perimenopause, or menopause transition, is the stage of a woman's reproductive life *that* begins several years before menopause, when the ovaries gradually begin to produce less estrogen. It usually starts in a woman's 40s, but can start in a woman's 30s or even earlier.

(https://www.webmd.com/menopause/guide/guide-perimenopause#1)

Perimenopause lasts up until menopause, the point when the ovaries stop releasing eggs. In the last one to two years of perimenopause, this decline in estrogen accelerates. At this stage, many women experience menopausal symptoms.

(https://www.webmd.com/menopause/guide/menopause-basics#1)

How Long Does Perimenopause Last? The average length of perimenopause is four years, but for some women this stage may last only a few months or continue for 10 years. Perimenopause ends the first year after the menopause (when a woman has gone 12 months without having a period).

(https://www.webmd.com/menopause/guide/guide-perimenopause#1)

There are between 20 to 66 symptoms of perimenopause (some of these symptoms may overlap) that a woman can experience. In this book I will walk you through my journey of a minimum of 12 different perimenopausal symptoms that affected me the most.

Note To Self

As you follow  through **Perimenopause**, please note that you too can take notes of your journey after each chapter to document your experience to see whether or not…

My Journey

"The Unexpected Season"

When I began having "weird" feelings and unexplainable crying I had a conversation with my doctor. Her response was "is there extreme stress in your life or some life changes in your family?" The only major change at that time was my daughter graduating from high school. Needless to say, my doctor was of no real help. But in my mind, I'm thinking that my daughter's graduation is not what's causing these unexplained crying spells.

Many women who are dealing with perimenopause rely on what their doctors' say. I'm not saying that you should not have this conversation with your doctor or that you should discontinue having checkups. But in my case, I was not receiving the definitive answers I was looking for, so I decided to rely on God and His word.

God made me in His image and He knows my body better than I do, therefore, I am trusting His word for comfort and strength (2 Corinthians 4:16) to help me during this season of perimenopause.

I take each day at a time and deal with whatever symptom may occur that day. I realized that by trying to look ahead and anticipate what will happen the next day, week, month, or years ahead I added more stress on myself. Scripture tells me to take no thought for tomorrow (Matthew 6:34).

Don't get me wrong, it took me a while to get to the point where I could say I am fully trusting and relying on God to help me through this journey of my life (and to be honest there were days where trusting God was in my heart and I knew it was the right thing to do, but the fog in my brain and my crazy emotional state did not want to agree).

I must admit there are times when I am so exhausted and overwhelmed by the episodes that I have to intentionally and audibly remind myself where my help comes from.

I initially was very frustrated and dejected. It was as if I was on a yo-yo string, not knowing from one minute to the next which direction to go, or which symptom would be thrown my way. One day my husband suggested we go to the Whole Food store to see what type of vitamins they had. There were a few to choose from.

I read the labels and bought what I thought was best for me. After about 4 months of taking the vitamins as described on the box, I didn't see any changes or feel any better. In my opinion, I was getting worse.

So, I threw the vitamins out! My frustration was heightened. I did more research and in the midst of my research the anxiety skyrocketed. Finally, in the middle of one of my violent crying spells I fell on my knees. My prayer was, "Father God in the Name of Jesus I don't know what to say. I'm experiencing something that I know every woman will one day experience, my relationship with my mother isn't the best so I really don't have anyone to call that has already experienced what I'm experiencing. Father you made me, you know more about me than I know about myself, your Word said that you even know the number of hairs on my head (Luke 12:7), your Word also says that you'll never leave me nor forsake me (Hebrews 13:5). You're a providential God; you're all seeing and all knowing. I'm surrendering myself to you Father in the Name of Jesus. I need your help! Please extend your mercy and give me grace to endure this journey of my life" (Lamentations 3:22-23). After I prayed I took a nap.

God did not answer me right away. And yes, I had other episodes in the interim. I remember vividly in the midst of an episode I began to get really agitated and my mind began to race (fear crept in). Almost as quickly as the agitation and mind racing began I felt a calmness overtake me. I began to verbally say, "Lord I need you," then I audibly heard, "take deep breaths; I'm here with you." Because I was home alone I knew His was the only voice I could be hearing and at that moment I knew my prayers were being answered. In my spirit I heard, "take each day, each episode at a time and in the midst of an episode verbally quote my Word."

Although the episodes were still very present, over time it was clear that God was giving me wisdom and strength to endure the episode. And He was working something out of me. His Word is true, God's grace is sufficient (2 Corinthians 12:9), even in the midst of an episode where I'm waiting for relief.

Even though I knew physiologically I wasn't exempt, when God showed me that my body was going through a change (perimenopause), as it will with all women, that wasn't comforting. The frustration and anger I was experiencing did not go away immediately. I kept saying to myself or should I say complaining to myself, (Phil 2:14) if I could just know when these episodes would happen I could prepare myself better. I must admit, I was dealing with **fear** (Psalm 34:4). Primarily, fear of the unknown, but at the time I didn't think I was. I was also dealing with **pride**, because if *I* knew when these episodes would occur then *I* could do something about it...or so I thought. I allowed the spirit of fear to enter into my mind (2 Timothy 1:7) and it opened up the door for the enemy to come in as well.

When the symptoms became more visible to me my mind became a battle field for the enemy. I began asking questions within myself and over-analyzing every change that occurred trying to get ahead of the next episode. I'm smart, I would say to myself, "once I start crying I'll be able to just shut it off." Ha! So, I thought.

God had other plans for me (Isaiah 55:8-9). God told me to look up perimenopause symptoms and only focus on the ones I was experiencing. I heard God loudly say, "don't focus on any symptom that you are not experiencing." I was disobedient because I wanted to know what symptoms I could possibly experience in the future so I would be prepared (that was fear creeping in). After reading and documenting the symptoms I was experiencing, I went on to read in detail the symptoms I wasn't experiencing.

My God, did I have to suffer for being disobedient. My stress level internally skyrocketed because I was so busy focusing in on what symptoms I could possibly get that the symptoms I did have seemed to be magnified 100%.

At this initial stage of my season of perimenopause my internal struggle was very difficult. By this time I was already emotionally and spiritually drained. But I trust God so I surrendered and asked God to forgive me. With the prayers of my husband (I thank God for my husband) and my surrender to God I was able to accept God's rebuke (Hebrews 12:6; Proverbs 3:12). From that point I was in a place to hear what God was telling me and take heed to His instructions (Proverbs 3:6).

Once I surrendered, I was able to accept and embrace this season of my life. Although some days are pretty challenging I remind myself that I have no control over my life anyway (Matthew 6:34; Romans 8:28; Jeremiah 29:11). Therefore, I must go on this journey of learning how to deal with perimenopause God's way. I want to reiterate, as I stated at the beginning that I am not advocating against going to your doctor, I went to my doctor.

Every woman's body is different and every woman will have different experiences during perimenopause. So, seek medical care if you desire to do so, but as Christians it is important to also seek God's guidance and use wisdom in your perimenopausal journey. As for me, I made a conscious and intentional decision to allow God and His Word to navigate me through this season of my life. Yes, I still go for my annual physical and mammogram; however, I am relying on God not medicine through this perimenopause journey so that I will have no doubts in trusting what He can and will do during my season of THE BIG M (menopause).

Entering the season of perimenopause can be emotionally, physically and spiritually draining. Chapter one will walk you through the onset of my first **"episode"** and my journey through perimenopause, thereafter each chapter will give you glimpses of my real-life experiences on my journey of 12 different perimenopausal episodes.

I pray that as you read my experiences the feeling of being alone will subside, the feeling that no one understands will diminish, and the truth that this season too shall pass will overshadow any dark or unexplainable days.

Chapter 1

The Crying Spell
(Mary Don't You Weep)

What is wrong with me?! I quickly mentally give myself a wellness check and immediately realized there is nothing physically wrong with me; my feelings didn't get hurt so why am I crying uncontrollably? When this first happened, it scared me because I didn't understand why I was crying and to boot I couldn't control the tears, they were streaming down my face as if someone turned on a faucet and forgot to turn it off. I would be off by myself and when my husband asked what was wrong, my answer was, "I don't know." I know this was probably very confusing for my family. They saw me crying but I couldn't tell them *why* I was crying. I felt horrible because I didn't know what was going on and I didn't have answers to give them. My husband initially thought it was related to some familial issues I had with my parents and thought I might be suffering from some emotions I hadn't dealt with. But I knew that wasn't the reason. After about an hour or so of this crying spell, my mind went to the reality of being 45 years old and back to some research I had done on perimenopause. So, I researched perimenopause symptoms again.

    What I initially found was a lot of clinical information. Although this was somewhat helpful, I needed something more practical that would explain these unwarranted crying spells that I was experiencing. The crying spells were really bad for about three months. After that time period they would resurface sporadically. Although I was no longer "bullied" by the crying spells, they were sometimes challenging to handle. (Not to mention all the new and different symptoms that began to happen to my body). Every time something new surfaced I documented it. Over time, I was able to compile the symptoms that were specific to me. (I will discuss those later). The symptoms would come on so quickly that I didn't have time to prepare for it.

    At the onset I wasn't experiencing symptoms every day, but at least 3-4 times per week I experienced both reoccurring and new symptoms. I became so frustrated not only because of the uncontrollable crying spells, but the other weird, unsolicited things that were happening to my body. I began to pray and ask God to show me what was wrong with me. Unbeknownst to me at that time, my husband was praying too! I thank God for a praying husband. I thought I had a handle on these crying spells, I thought I could control them because they had started to decrease. Ha! Boy, was I wrong.   I went through another season of crying spells.

PEARL TO PONDER:

These rubber boots are a reminder that God is here to help us during the worst storms. No matter how much it rains, rain boots are designed to keep our feet dry. Also, the rubber duck may bob up and down but it will always stay afloat. So in the midst of your crying season remember God is with you to help you stay afloat. *(Isaiah 43:2; Psalms 6:1)*

Self-Reflection

Fill in the blank: Today I am experiencing an episode of_____, but I will not allow this episode to overtake me because I am choosing to_____.

Chapter 1 NOTES

My Crying Spells

AHHHHH!!! I Can't Take This Anymore!

Chapter 2

Fatigue, Sleepiness, and Exhaustion

(Can You Not Watch for One Hour?)

Sometimes, this hits me like a ton of bricks. I can be fine one minute and the next it seems like I haven't slept or rested in days. Let me explain the difference. When I get sleepy, I will sleep on and off all day. If I sit down I will fall asleep.

Fatigue is when my body feels as if someone has beaten it continually with a baseball bat, I'm so tired that I can't sleep or rest. Exhaustion is a combination of being sleepy and fatigued, this is when I sleep the hardest but only for short periods of time. If I awake for any reason, it is difficult for me to fall back into an uninterrupted state of sleep. Although my eyes are closed, I am not in a restful state physically or mentally.

I never have a problem going to sleep, my issue is staying asleep. I usually don't get a full night of sleep which contributes to me being sleepy, fatigued and exhausted. I have the opportunity during the day to sleep when I'm in these states, but often when I try I can only actually sleep for about half an hour at a time, which makes me even more tired.

Usually, I just lay there and rest but this can be counterproductive, because the frustration of not being able to actually sleep is also exhausting.

Dealing with sleepiness/fatigue/exhaustion can be frustrating for your spouse. There were times when my husband would be talking to me and I would fall asleep. When he asked me if I was asleep I would say, "no" initially not realizing that I was falling asleep in the middle of a conversation. Although I felt extremely bad about falling asleep while he was talking, the effort it took to stay awake was exhausting. I finally talked to my husband about the frustration I was experiencing. I told him when the sleepy/fatigue/exhaustion episode happens I need to go to sleep at that moment. He understood.

Much to my surprise that method helps to some degree. The sleepiness/fatigue/exhaustion haven't totally disappeared but I am not as frustrated when this episode occurs. I learned to shut everything down, quiet myself and try to get in a relaxed state of being mentally, emotionally and physically. Honestly, I believe it was my husband's prayers that gave me relief (Proverbs 3:24; Psalms 4:8).

PEARL TO PONDER:

When in this episode, everything can become so convoluted due to sheer tiredness. Your life can appear to be an intertwined ball of moods and emotions, leaving you a tangled mess. However, think about the *focus* and *time* it takes to create a rubber band ball. Use the image of the rubber band ball as a reminder for us to focus and take time to make ourselves relax. God said He will give us sweet rest if our minds are stayed on Him (Proverbs 3:24). So, during this episode, although it may seem impossible, *focus* and *take time* to intentionally rest your body, mind and soul, just as someone intentionally focuses and takes time to create the rubber band ball for the purpose of relaxation.

Self-Reflection

Fill in the blank: Today I am experiencing an episode of_____, but I will not allow this episode to overtake me because I am choosing to _____.

AHHHHH!!! I Can't Take This Anymore!

My Fatigue, Sleepiness, and Exhaustion

Anger and Rage

(Contentious Are You?)

This is a new one for me and it caught me off guard because I am usually a very calm person. But when this episode hits me, always without warning, internally I feel as if I'm on fire. There is not one thing (at least at this point) that I have pinpointed that triggers the anger and rage. I was sitting at my kitchen table one day looking out the window watching a squirrel and all of a sudden, I felt myself getting angry. What is it about a squirrel that could possibly make me angry? Was the enemy upset that I was marveling at God's creation and meditating on His goodness?

As I was sitting at the table I physically felt the anger and rage rising as if someone had poured hot water in my body. I looked down at my hands and they were balled into fists. There was a war going on in my mind, I began quoting, "we wrestle not against flesh and blood but principalities" (Ephesians 6:12).

"Think on things that are lovely" (Philippians 4:8). In the middle of me verbally quoting God's Word the enemy kept trying to inundate and overtake my mind trying to convince me that something was wrong with me. The more I breathed the angrier I became.

I had become so angry that I felt like destroying

something (this internal rage unexpectedly happened on several occasion). I continued to breathe, audibly I said, "there is nothing wrong with me. I am not sick nor am I under any pressure." I repeated the scriptures while doing an internal wellness check to see if something happened or was said that could have made me angry, but that was not the case.

After repeating the scriptures several times, I gave God thanks, "Father in The Name of Jesus, I thank you for giving me this time to observe your creation (remember the squirrel) and view how he is accomplishing the purpose you have for his life. The enemy wanted to destroy the solitude time I was spending with you by magnifying a symptom that is part of my physical journey of being a woman, not just a woman but a woman that you created for a purpose. Thank you for the Holy Spirit that guided me through this episode and the promises of your Word." Immediately, I felt the hotness of the anger begin to subside.

I must admit, this was not the last episode of anger and rage. But I now understand how to use God's Word to cope with the episode to not leave room for the enemy to overtake my mind during that time. This episode is very frustrating for me because I am by nature a calm person, however, when this episode occurs the battle is real and intense. The weirdest thing about this episode is that it happens more often when I am by myself than it does when I am in the presence of other people. This episode of rage/anger prompted me to the PMS article listed at the end of this book.

PEARL TO PONDER:

This firecracker picture is a reminder of the potentially volatile action or reactions that can occur during this episode that can lead to a lot of danger if not harnessed. It is also a reminder to not allow the sun to go down on our wrath (Ephesians 4:26) and to look to the hills from whence cometh our help (Psalms 121:1-2). Regardless of how angry you are in this season God is still in control (Psalm 139).

Self-Reflection

Fill in the blank: Today I am experiencing an episode of_____, but I will not allow this episode to overtake me because I am choosing to _____.

My Anger and Rage

Chapter 4

Nausea and Queasiness

(If I Could Just Touch…)

For me, this episode was normal PMS on steroids. I just had to get used to the frequency and randomness of the episodes. When I experience the nausea alone I have a sour stomach with no desire to eat. The queasiness makes my mouth extremely watery but my tongue was dry. When they occur at the same time the sensation of the loss of my taste buds increases, my smell senses became heightened and smells that didn't affect me before now became more prevalent and intensifies the queasiness.

The majority of everyday sweet smells became unpleasant and made me nauseated and queasy. Food also became an issue for me when this episode occurs. I lose all taste for food during this time. (No, this does *not* cause me to lose weight! LOL). Although I thought at the time these symptoms should be fairly easy to deal with, it was actually a playground for the enemy to come in and attack my mind. On several occasions I had a battle in my head. It went like this:

Enemy: You know if you don't eat you'll get a headache.

Me: Okay, well I'll just eat a sandwich.

Enemy: You know if you eat too much lunchmeat it might raise your sodium level. Remember you had

Vertigo? Oh you don't want to pass out again do you?

The conversation went like that in my head about the different negative effect's food had on me over my life, watch your sodium levels, certain foods increase cholesterol, causes bloating…you get the point. As I stood in my kitchen with the refrigerator door wide open I took a deep breath and verbally quoted God's Word, "let this mind be in you which is also in Christ Jesus" (Philippians 2:5). I said, "Father in The Name of Jesus, you made me and you know my body better than I do." I closed the refrigerator door and walked out of the kitchen.

The nausea and queasiness symptoms haven't changed, actually sometimes they seem to have gotten worse, but *how I viewed the symptoms* changed. If I eat, I eat, If I don't, I don't. When I smell something unpleasant, I try to relieve the smell with the scent of lemon, cinnamon or ginger. Chewing gum or crushed ice sometimes gives me temporary relief, but for the most part I just have to ride it out. I begin to think on things that are lovely to try to take my mind off the negative feeling I get from this episode.

PEARL TO PONDER:

When this awful sickening episode arises, remember God is there to take care of us (Matthew 6:25-34). Think about the journey of a butterfly and the process it goes through to become one of God's beautiful creatures. Although you may not feel beautiful during this episode, the butterfly represents how beautiful and wonderful God has made you (Psalm 138:14).

Self-Reflection

Fill in the blank: Today I am experiencing an episode of_____, but I will not allow this episode to overtake me because I am choosing to _____.

AHHHHH!!! I Can't Take This Anymore!

My Nausea and Queasiness

_____
_____
_____
_____
_____
_____
_____
_____
_____
_____
_____
_____
_____
_____
_____
_____
_____
_____
_____
_____

Headaches and Migraines

(Momentary Affliction = Glory Beyond Compassion)

AHHHHH!!! I Can't Take This Anymore!

I went through a two-month period where I was taking Advil, Aleve and/or Tylenol every single day in an attempt to relieve the headaches I was experiencing. Nothing I did seemed to trigger it or bring relief. I tried different foods and natural remedies, but to no avail. The severity of the headache changed from hour to hour, ranging from that small nagging, annoying headache to a pounding headache that made me nauseated and altered my mood.

When this episode occurred the smallest sound, even the sound of a text message, irritated me.

Sitting at my kitchen table, as I often do, my head in my hands with a pounding headache (after taking Advil) I closed my eyes and envisioned myself lying in the arms of God. As I am envisioning lying in God's arms, the enemy is whispering in my ear, "call your husband you need to go to the hospital, something is really wrong." Tears are streaming down my face because I'm in so much pain. I didn't call my husband.

Instead, I began to internally complain about going through perimenopause and not having anyone to talk to and having my own full-blown pity party. Yes while envisioning lying in the arms of God. In the midst of my pity party, and tears, the sound of a text comes in (remember, that sound that irritated me). At the same time I heard the voice of The Lord say, "the season you're in now and the journey you're on is not for you, it is to help someone else." Oh, the text. When my husband is not home and I'm having an episode he always seems to know when to send an uplifting text. His text said, "I love you, and what you are going through is to help someone else. You have a calling to help women, use your experiences to minister to others."

Initially, my flesh didn't want to receive either the voice of The Lord or my husband's text. But I yielded to the Holy Spirit, took a deep breath and said to myself, "His grace is sufficient" (2 Corinthians 12:9). Yes, the headaches still occur, but because I know God's grace is sufficient (2 Corinthians 12:9) I have learned (actually I am still learning) to be content and manage the range of pain (Philippians 4:11-12). As soon as I became content in learning to manage the pain of the headaches, even to the point where some days the headache was not noticeable, then *bam*, out of nowhere December 2017 I began to experience migraines. WOW! At first, I thought they were just headaches like I had experienced before and that they would eventually go away. But the over the counter pain medication I was taking daily was not doing the job. In fact, it seemed as if the pain medication was making the headache worse. I had a migraine every day, all day, for one month. The migraines were getting so bad it caused vertigo to flare up and at that point my daily activities were hampered.

On January 3, 2018 I could not get out of bed. My husband took me to the ER, I was treated and regained some relief. But while I was there one doctor matter of factually stated, "oh, you could be experiencing perimenopause migraines." Although in pain, my eyebrow went up. Immediately, I began to have an internal anxiety attack. Fear crept in and all I could think about was that there was no way I would be able to function with migraines. There I was again, saying what *I* would not be able to do. Once I was able to look at a computer screen without being in pain, I did my own research. Sure enough, with fear looming, I found some information on perimenopause migraines. Then I went right into what *I* needed to do to try to prevent the migraines from happening. But, my God! As always, He steps in right on time. After taking a dose of the medicine I was prescribed, I heard loud and clear (I was home alone so I know it was God speaking to my spirit), "I don't care how much research you do, what foods you eat or do not eat, I am in control of what happens to your body" (Jeremiah 1:5).

PEARL TO PONDER:

    We all know how hard, yet fragile, an eggshell is. It has the potential to crack at the slightest touch. During this episode you might feel as if your head that is hard to the touch will crack at the slightest touch or sound. Just like the outer shell is the protector of what's inside, God is our protector and will comfort us during this episode. But we must remember to walk in the fear of the Lord and allow God to do the rest (Psalm 91: 1-4).

Self-Reflection

Fill in the blank: Today I am experiencing an episode of_____, but I will not allow this episode to overtake me because I am choosing to_____.

AHHHHH!!! I Can't Take This Anymore!

My Headaches and Migraines

Chapter 6

*Night Sweats,
Hot Flashes and Freezing Cold*

(Please Don't Spew Me Out)

As far back as I can remember, I have been sleeping in socks or footies regardless of the temperature. I hear the jokes and comments all the time about "hot flashes." Up to this point, I have not fully experienced a hot flash. But I am experiencing night sweats and cold sweats. When I'm experiencing a night sweat the inside of my elbows, the back of my knees, my head and hair, between my toes, my back, under my breast, and behind my ears, began to sweat profusely. I would take off one sock, then immediately my entire body feels as if I have been dipped into a tub filled with subzero water. Not only is this very irritating, but it disrupts my sleep.

In the midst of one of these episodes the scripture came to mind, "The Lord will rather have you hot or cold not lukewarm" (Revelation 3:15-16). When these episodes occur, it is a welcomed reminder for me to check myself to see if I'm hot or cold in my service to God, if I am allowing those little foxes to creep in (Song of Solomon 2:15), or if I'm holding bitterness or unforgiveness in my heart (Ephesians 4:31-33).

Although the night sweats and cold sweats are very uncomfortable I accept them now without complaint because they are constant reminders to check myself so that I don't become lukewarm. If I do find myself in a state of cold complacency I need to repent and seek God's forgiveness.

Oh, remember at the onset of this section I said I had not experienced hot flashes. Well, on September 18, 2017 that certainly changed and all I could say is "WOW!" Out of nowhere, this intense heat permeated the inside of my body as if I walked into an ancient wood fire oven that originated in Greece. All I felt was internal heat and sweat. At that moment, I knew what it meant and how it felt when women would say, "I'm having a personal summer." It is hard to explain. I thought the night sweats and cold sweats were uncomfortable, but my level of uncomfortableness has magnified 100%.

However, in all of that I am quickly reminded that the hot flashes I experience do not compare to the hot flashes I would endure if I am not living my life according to God's Word. When a hot flash occurs I often find myself giving God praise at that moment, however uncomfortable or irritating they maybe. I do not want to find myself standing before God and have him cast me into outer darkness and my soul spending eternity in the Lake of Fire (Matthew 7:23, 25:30). So, I humbly endure the dreaded hot flashes and I tell myself this too, one day, shall pass.

PEARL TO PONDER: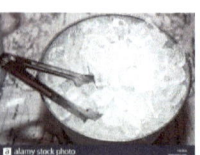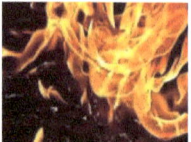

Cold and hot are polar temperature opposites. During these episodes there seems to be no middle ground of comfort. But I'm often reminded what Jesus said, "I would rather have you hot or cold but because you're lukewarm I'll spew you out of my mouth" (Revelation 3:15-16). This inspires me to make sure I have a right relationship with Christ and to continue growing in His grace (2 Peter 3:8).

Self-Reflection

Fill in the blank: Today I am experiencing an episode of _____, but I will not allow this episode to overtake me because I am choosing to _____.

Chapter 6 NOTES

My Night Sweats, Hot Flashes and Freezing Cold

Chapter 7

Stress Incontinence

(Is That The Water of Life?)

I know, I know, who wants to talk about "it" (leakage). But it happens and when it happens what do you do? What goes through your mind? For me, when it first happened I was doing jumping jacks. It caught me off guard. My initial thought was, "is that what I think it is?" The first time, I dismissed it. It wasn't a lot so no big deal. I began to notice that "it" happened if I jumped, ran, sneezed or coughed hard. So, I talked to my doctor. She said matter of factually, *"oh, it's nothing to worry about you have stress incontinence."* She gave me some Kegel exercises to do and said if it gets worse I can have surgery.

After starting the Kegel exercises I initially thought it was getting better. To be honest though, as far as the Kegel exercises go, I can't say how well they work because I have not done them consistently. I know my personal doctor and my doctor friends told me that they work well to help reduce or eliminate stress incontinence, but the truth of the matter is even after being shown demonstrations I am not sure if I am doing the exercise correctly. Anyway, there is still leakage from time to time.

Now I'm not at the point where I need special undergarments, however I am conscious that it does happen. I either am able to catch myself and prevent it by running to the bathroom, crossing my legs, squeezing my vaginal muscles really tight, or wearing a panty liner. I must admit there have been times when I have been caught off guard...thank God I was at home and able to change my undergarments. Scripture tells me in all things give thanks (1 Thessalonians 5:18) and I am thankful for stress incontinence being the least of my symptoms, I dread to think if this was an everyday all-day occurrence.

PEARL TO PONDER:

The flowers in this pot are so pretty. But no one sees what goes on in the space between the base of the pot and the dirt in the pot. As women who are experiencing this episode, we look so pretty on the outside, but no one knows what's going on in the spaces they can't see, and truthfully, we don't want anyone to know. But just like the pretty flowers need water to survive, if too much water is taken in, there needs to be somewhere for the water to escape.

I do not want my water to escape unassisted, and neither do you. However, I use this example for us to focus on the beauty of where we are at during this stage of life and how some women would love to trade places with us. Yes, this episode can be uncomfortable and embarrassing for some, but give God thanks (1Thessalonias 5:18) anyway because it could be worse.

Self-Reflection

Fill in the blank: Today I am experiencing an episode of_____, but I will not allow this episode to overtake me because I am choosing to _____.

AHHHHH!!! I Can't Take This Anymore!

Chapter 7 NOTES

My Stress Incontinence

Chapter 8

Bloating and Weight gain

(In Spite of, I'm Still God's Handiwork)

This bloating thing really got me. I have never bloated in my life (even during that time of the month). Then one day, out of the blue, it looked as if I was in my first trimester of pregnancy. My mind immediately began to review what I had eaten in the last two days. Nothing came to mind that would have caused excessive bloating. The bloating battle began and has remained a constant fight. Oh, and its best friend *weight gain* is close by.

I never had a problem with my weight, and never "had" to work out (although I should have). I'm 5" 3 ½ and was always able to keep my weight under 125 lbs. My husband used to say, "how can anyone eat just one chip out of a bag?" But, I did. Unfortunately, when the bloating started so did the weight gain. I eat fairly healthy. I'm not a big junk food eater. So, I'm asking myself what am I eating that's causing this weight gain? Ahhhh! It's a perimenopause thing. At the time I began documenting this journey I had gained about 20-25 pounds. Just saying that brings stress. And this mid-section weight is very stubborn and hard to get rid of. Although I have taken yoga and exercise classes and I try to walk at least 3-4 times per week, staying on a consistent exercise routine is very challenging because I am constantly hindered by debilitating headaches.

I know as I get older my body is changing and weight gain and weight shifts will occur. One thing I have learned during this episode of bloating and weight gain is that if I stress out about it and keep looking at the scale, I'll gain more weight**. And the most important thing I stopped doing was comparing myself to other women!** I prayed and asked God to give me peace about this portion of my journey. I know it's easier said than done, but as long as I am healthy I won't complain about my weight. In whatever state I'm in, I choose to be content (Philippines 4:11). No, that doesn't mean I will just throw my hands up and say, "forget it." I am continuing to eat healthy and do some form of exercise.

January 2016, this bloating was way out of control. I would tell my husband how "full" I felt all the time. It was as if someone had injected me with air. January 10, 2016 we were sitting in the basement watching TV. I was extremely uncomfortable. He finally looked at my stomach and said, "wow!"

At that moment he realized the seriousness of what I had been saying. Being the loving husband that he is, he immediately went into prayer. After praying and some research, we came to the conclusion I should remove all dairy from my diet.

Not only was I severely bloated, I was constipated-- yeah I said it! From January 2016 through June 2016 my elimination was little to none and when I could go it was extremely hard. It got to the point where I just did not want to go. So, I went to my doctor. I was put on a Phillips Milk of Magnesia for two weeks along with Benefiber. Even after this trip to the doctor and trying the prescribed supplements I still had little to no relief. So I tried a few natural remedies. Baking soda, which made me sick. Black strap molasses, which seemed to work really well for several weeks until the constipation and lack of elimination returned. I was sent to see a GI doctor and had a colonoscopy. Everything was fine. So, the culprit perimenopause temporally won this round.

I continued to watch what I ate. Reintroducing oatmeal helped with the bloating initially, but the bloating soon returned. I did some form of exercise at least three times a week. I reminded myself again that, this too shall pass. It's only a season (2 Corinthians 4:15-18).

Nausea, nausea, nausea! This symptom seems to want to hang on as if it's my Siamese twin. As I'm changing my diet and eliminating certain foods altogether, nausea is my biggest challenge in this area. I was put on Omeprazole and Ondansetron ODT for nausea, but I just did not want to be relegated to having to take medication daily prior to eating a meal. So, after a little research I decided to not drink any liquid half an hour prior to and half an hour after any meal. The reasoning is the acid in your stomach is what helps to break down food for proper digestion and if you drink liquids is dilutes the acid therefore hindering the proper breakdown of how the food is supposed to be digested.

    I started that routine April 2018 and it was working fine until I went to Mexico July 2018. The old nausea came back. So now I am left to decipher if the current nausea is related to the Montezuma's Revenge or perimenopause. Unfortunately, when the nausea sticks around like it is, it is very challenging to eat or even smell food. But I keep quoting, "God, you gave me this body, you know it better that I do, (Psalm 139:2) so whatever is causing the nausea I ask if you don't reveal and remove it that you give me the grace, peace and the wherewithal to withstand it" (2 Corinthians 12:9). In all things give thanks! (1 Thessalonians 5:18).

PEARL TO PONDER:

A braided cord can become very tight and uncomfortable and sometimes difficult to unbraid. When in this episode we too may feel very tight and uncomfortable not knowing when or if relief will occur. But remember no matter how much discomfort we may experience God loved us enough to send His son Jesus to redeem us of our sins (John 3:16). Let's not forget the many uncomfortable situations Jesus endured and the fact that the Holy Spirit was sent back as our comforter (John 16:7) to comfort us in any area where we are feeling discomfort or distress.

Self-Reflection

Fill in the blank: Today I am experiencing an episode of_____, but I will not allow this episode to overtake me because I am choosing to _____.

Chapter 8 NOTES

My Bloating and Weight gain

Chapter 9

Joint Pains and Boobs On Fire

(I Won't Let Go Until You Bless Me)

In 2012 I began having pain in my right shoulder. I initially attributed it to picking up groceries or laundry baskets. But as the days went on not only did the pain increase and intensify, I began to lose strength and mobility. My shoulder would literally lock up. I went to my primary care doctor and she thought it had something to do with my nerves. I had several neck and spine X-rays and took steroid pills. I went to physical therapy and a chiropractor; all to no avail.

Increasingly, I needed help for simple day to day necessities like putting on or taking off clothes. After almost a year of debilitating pain and loss of mobility I was sent to a specialist.

To make a long story short, he said I have Impingement and Adhesive Capsulitis. I know I must have had a puzzled look on my face. The thought that went through my mind was, "what is that?" To put it in simple terms, I had frozen shoulder and adhesions around the cap of my shoulder. At that point I really didn't care what the clinical terms was. All I wanted to know is how to get the pain to go away and have full range and mobility restored to my shoulder.

I had surgery May 2013. All went well and I was

pain free with great mobility. Yeah! But the celebration was cut short. Less than six months later I began to experience the same symptoms in my right shoulder accompanied by an achy weird feeling, needless to say I did not wait a year to have surgery. This surgery happened by February 2014.

All went well with the surgery, but that achy weird feeling shows up every now and then. I was cleaning my closet out one day and came across the sling I had to wear after one of the shoulder surgeries. I just stared at it for a moment. I heard the word "dependent." I audibly began to say, "dependent" multiple times. Then in my spirit I heard, "just as you were dependent on that sling to help with the healing process of your shoulder surgery, you need to become more conscientious and intentional about your (my) dependency on God." All I could say is, "Wow!" I thanked God for the conviction and praised Him for loving me enough to convict me (Hebrews 12:6-11).

Often times God will allow certain ailments to happen in our bodies to slow us down so that we can refocus on Him not for what He can, has, or will do, but for who He *is* in all His glory. I thought about how dependent I was on my family during my shoulder issues and it made me reflect on if I am allowing myself to have that same unwavering dependence on God and trusting His Word without question.

November 2015, I began to have this burning sensation around the nipples of my breast. It didn't hurt to touch, but the sensation was so deeply embedded in my breast that I didn't know what to think. All I knew was my breast felt like fire; here I go again with another one of those symptoms. I didn't complain, but I had to fight off fear (1 Timothy 1:7). The enemy tried to whisper that something serious was wrong, maybe I had cancer. I didn't panic. I didn't rush to call my doctor. It took me about a week to even research to see what it could possibly be. Once I did, I realized it was just another one of those symptoms and a slight smile came on my face.

You're probably asking how can I smile while experiencing all these different symptoms of perimenopause, some of which can be very difficult to deal with. The moment the smile came on my face I was reminded of how sovereign God is and no matter what my body may be experiencing I can always find comfort in His Word. The physical symptoms may still be present but through it all I'm learning to have a quiet and calm spirit (1 Peter 3:4).

The beginning of 2016, I began having nagging irritation in my hips, especially my right hip. At first, I didn't think too much about it and just carried on with life as normal.

But over time the nagging irritation began to turn into pain, not pain to the touch, or when I walk, just pain. Then the pain was accompanied by restricted movement.

This became extremely frustrating because it caused me to alter how I do things. I continued to pray, I even had an x-ray in September 2016 which came out fine. The enemy started telling me I would need hip surgery. I said so loud one day, "LIES!" Whatever was going on with my hip I literally put it in God's hands. I had to alter my exercises due to the pain and began to stretch only. The pain didn't totally go away but the severity and length of the pain has decreased, I even went through a period of about 6 months in 2018 where I had no pain. Thank you Jesus!

PEARL TO PONDER:

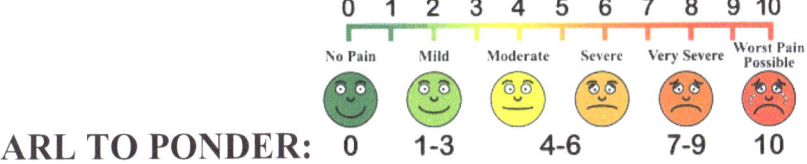

We all at some point have been to the doctor where we have seen this picture or the doctor asks you, "on a scale of 1-10 what is your pain level?" As our bodies age it is guaranteed that we will experience pain to some degree. All pain will not be eliminated from our bodies, but the severity of your pain will not always be the same. God's grace is sufficient (2 Corinthians 12:9). Use this pain scale as a reminder to keep your focus on God and remember that He will never leave you nor forsake you (Hebrews 13:5) and to trust God and lean not to your own understanding (Proverbs 3:5-6).

Self-Reflection

Fill in the blank: Today I am experiencing an episode of_____, but I will not allow this episode to overtake me because I am choosing to_____.

AHHHHH!!! I Can't Take This Anymore!

My Joint Pains and Boobs On Fire

Chapter 10

Digestive Issues
(The Jonah Experience)

AHHHHH!!! I Can't Take This Anymore!

January 2015 is when the chest pains first started. I thought I might have pulled a muscle, but the pain didn't feel muscular. I also felt discomfort in my throat. The pain continued to worsen, my energy level was decreasing, sleeping was difficult and my breathing was taxing. What is happening?! All types of thoughts were running through my mind. Even though it was becoming increasingly challenging, I continued to go about my days as normal.

After about a week or so, the pain wasn't ceasing so my husband took me to the ER. They ran every type of test possible to rule out any issues with my heart. Praise God they all came back negative. One of the attending doctors haphazardly asked me if I was going through perimenopause, I said, "yes" but he said nothing more about it, he just walked out of the room. I was in pain and had so much discomfort that I didn't put any thought into his statement. Eventually, they sent me home telling me to follow up with my primary doctor. When I did, she referred me to a heart specialist.

To make a long story short, the specialist examined me, put me on a heart monitor and did the stress test. Everything came back negative; she even ruled out angina. The diagnosis was severe acid reflux, but not directly related to food. You can probably imagine the look on my face when I heard that report. So February 2015, my doctor prescribed Omeprazole for 6 months. I didn't like how it made me feel, so by faith I stopped taking the medicine after one month. *****Please note: I am simply sharing my own personal experience. I am not advocating that anyone stop taking medication prescribed by a physician***** My decision to stop the medication prescribed by my physician was based on the faith I have in God being a healer in my life. This act of faith was due to other situations where He has healed my body, and I clearly heard the voice of the Lord telling me to trust Him (Proverbs 3:5-6).

AHHHHH!!! I Can't Take This Anymore!

PEARL TO PONDER:

Imagine what soda pop cans must feel like when shaken; or Jonah as he sat in the belly of the great fish. Internally there's pressure, expansion, bubbles that rise, fizz, then *BOOM*--the explosion. Although you may feel like these soda pop cans during this episode, there is always some relief after the explosion. In spite of how our bodies feel, God wants us to trust Him. God often allows aliments to occur to get our attention. So, during this episode season refocus and renew your mind daily (Romans 12:2). Every time you feel pressure, expansion, bubbles rising, and fizz, let that be a reminder to renew your mind.

Self-Reflection

Fill in the blank: Today I am experiencing an episode of _____, but I will not allow this episode to overtake me because I am choosing to _____.

My Digestive Issues

AHHHHH!!! I Can't Take This Anymore!

Decreased Motor Coordination and Clumsiness
(So, That's Funny To You?)

All I can do is laugh. You're probably wondering, why am I laughing at having decreased motor coordination and clumsiness? My laughter comes from all of the situations where I audibly ask myself, "How did that just happen?"

Let me give you some examples. It seems like every time I go in and out of my closet, I manage to hit my elbow or shoulder on the doorway. I have fallen up the stairs on multiple occasion (no my hands were not full). Many times I've almost slipped off the step ladder getting something out of the kitchen cabinets. Then there was the whopper of them all: me falling out of my backdoor December 2015. I went to grab the screen door to close it and the next thing I knew I was on my knees hanging over the railing. When I tried to get up all I felt was excruciating pain. The end result was a severely sprained ankle and foot. I was on crutches and had to wear a brace for six weeks. When I think about it now I still shake my head and say, "how did that happen?" Needless to say, every time I go out or come in the back door I am *very* careful. Can you see now why I just have to laugh?

My senses are heightened by the mishaps that have

occurred during these episodes. Plus, I'm getting a greater appreciation for how God has meticulously woven our bodies together, and the intricacies of how each part of our bodies work independently, yet interdependently upon each other. It might sound trivial to some, but I often internally say Lord guide my steps...meaning *literally* guide my feet.

I'm laughing because a thought just came to mind. Sometimes when my young adult children and I are together and I'm experiencing one of these episodes, they'll look at each other then look at me and say, "ma what is wrong with you, we need to help you work on your balance." All I do is laugh then I attempt to show them one of my yoga poses.

PEARL TO PONDER:

A bar of soap has positive and negative effects and is designed to be used for multiple purposes. An initial bar of soap can be hard and sturdy, however over time that same bar of soap can begin to shrink and become fragile to the point where it's original intent no longer serves its purpose. Our bodies are like a bar of soap. So as our bodies progress into different stages of our lives we need to be cognizant of its frailty, yet reminded of God's grace and mercy (Lamentations 3:22-23) that He allows us to enjoy the sturdy times of our lives and because He allowed us to enjoy the sturdy season of our lives we too must be grateful and enjoy every minute of the season of frailty of our lives. Life is but a vapor (James 4:14) let's live until we die.

Self-Reflection

Fill in the blank: Today I am experiencing an episode of_____, but I will not allow this episode to overtake me because I am choosing to_____.

AHHHHH!!! I Can't Take This Anymore!

My Decreased Motor Coordination and Clumsiness

Chapter 12

Increased Hair Loss and Thinning (CCCA)
(Jesus How Many Hairs Do I Have?)

July 2013, is when I noticed my hair thinning at the crown. So, I did what most women do when their hair is thinning, I went natural. No perm, I simply had a dark rinse put in my hair every six weeks. I was of the mindset that all I needed to do to my hair in its natural state was moisturize/oil my scalp more often because it was dry. I even took it a step further and began taking vitamins that are specifically formulated for hair health. But other than those two steps, I didn't put too much effort into the health of my hair or scalp because I thought it was just a phase and it would grow back. Boy, was I in denial!

During my three-year phase of being natural I noticed the thinning at the crown was not getting any better. In my mind at the time, I thought being natural would cure the thinning. Finally, out of frustration of not knowing how to take care of natural hair, I went back to the perm. My stylist was skilled at making my hair look great despite the thinning, and I kept wearing camouflaging styles. I asked her professional opinion on whether the thinning was getting any better, hoping she would tell me what I wanted to hear, instead of what I knew to be true. She told me if there is something wrong with my scalp there is nothing she could do. I heard her but

I didn't take action for almost six months. I was in denial.

I had dealt with an extremely painful scalp for years to the point it made my head ache; but it just became a way of life for me and I never talked about it. After much prayer and some research, I decided to get out of denial and see a dermatologist. On June 19, 2017 I was diagnosed with Central Centrifugal Cicatricial Alopecia (CCCA—Scarring Alopecia) and Traction Alopecia (TA), both caused by hair practices that are damaging to the scalp (i.e. pressing, perms, weave, braids, tight and prolonged up styles, rollers, hot oil, hood and blow dryers) as well as Seborrheic Dermatitis (SD) a common inflammatory skin condition where one of the leading factors is oily skin and excessive growth of normal yeast.

Although I was kind of prepared for the worst, the diagnosis was still a shock and a blow to my self-esteem. As I sat in the doctor's office I heard a still small voice saying, "your self-esteem may be taking a blow now, but I will get the glory in the end. You will use this blow to your self-esteem to witness who I am."

This journey may not be easy, and I don't know if my hair will grow in the crown of my head where the follicles were severely damaged, but it is making me revisit my faith in God and trust that He knows what is best for me. Although my diagnoses related to hair loss and thinning are not directly due to the hormonal changes of perimenopause, hair loss and thinning can be symptoms of perimenopause. If you are experiencing hair loss and thinning, don't wait and be in denial as I was. Go see a dermatologist to rule out any damage to your scalp, because if your scalp isn't healthy then your hair will not be healthy.

As women our hair is our crown and if you are anything like I was, my hair had to be laid all the time. But my diagnosis was a wake-up call. I did not realize that my hair had become my god (Exodus 20:3). This wake-up call allowed me to begin to see myself as God sees me regardless of what was going on with my hair. I had to become okay with seeing myself differently than how the world and friends saw me. I began to quote "I am fearfully and wonderfully made" (Psalm 139:14), and "God you know the number of hairs on my head" (Luke 12:7). So regardless of how many hairs I have, or don't have, I asked God to give me a peace about this diagnosis and let me see Him within myself when I look in the mirror.

I must be honest, during the first year after my diagnosis I had some challenging days, weeks, and months where I did not feel beautiful. It took time and prayer to become at peace with myself. The enemy wanted to hold this area of my life over my head and make me feel bad about myself, but all I can say is, *"but God."*

God put in my path women who were experiencing what I was experiencing (if not worse), and gave me an opportunity to share my story. The tears that were shared by other women who said I was courageous, and the confidence I gave other women (unbeknownst to me) to go see a dermatologist and stop the hair practices that were causing hair and scalp damage was a humbling experience. So, with that being said, as I stated earlier this symptom may not be directly related to perimenopause, but like symptoms of perimenopause it can be very challenging; to the point where it can emotionally, spiritually and physically change who you are as a woman. Once again I say, *"but God"* because I know without a shadow of a doubt that if I did not have a personal relationship with Christ, and if I did not seek God's Word for comfort, direction, grace and peace, I would not be able to share my journey with you. Apart from Him, I would have folded and succumbed to the weight of the symptoms, becoming bitter instead of better.

Seasons come and go. We think we know the type of weather the season will bring, yet a twist happens and something out of the ordinary for that season occurs. So it is with journeys in our lives. Some journeys are well planned out and others happen without notice. But one thing for sure when you are on your life's journey, something unexpected is bound to happen and it's your *perspective* on the unexpected that will determine the outcome and have a positive or negative effect on your mental health.

PEARL TO PONDER:

Oftentimes in life as women we look at, or to, other women to see if we measure up in terms of fashion, weight, hair styles, careers, parenting, etc. Sometimes we think the grass in their yard is better so we try to acclimate to their way of doing or being, but this can become detrimental to our own mental and sometimes physical health.

This *PEARL TO PONDER* is a reminder that when it is all said and done, we are accountable to God for our own lives, and for how well we nurture the seeds He has planted in us in order for them to flourish so that He gets the glory (1 Corinthians 3:5-10).

Self-Reflection

Fill in the blank: Today I am experiencing an episode of_____, but I will not allow this episode to overtake me because I am choosing to _____.

My Increased Hair Loss and Thinning (CCCA)

Chapter 13

My Husband's Perspective of My Journey
(Covenant Love)

Throughout this journey I often wonder how my husband is emotionally doing and what he would say to help men navigate life during this season. I no longer need to speculate on his perspective and I get to share with you his thoughts and feelings of how he is dealing with me and my journey through perimenopause.

Pastor Tracy Jennings shares:

I had to fight against the fear associated with wondering if my wife was no longer interested in me or if she was seeing someone else. This thought process was due to my wife's dramatic mood changes and the fact that initially, she was not able to explain what she was going through. So I was left to speculate. But prayer helped me because it prevented me from becoming accusatory, although that was my first reaction. Once my wife was able to explain what was happening and the changes she was experiencing, it developed another form of intimacy. I realized the importance of learning together, understanding the process, and taking it one step at a time.

After some time I was able to recognize the patterns of some episodes. As men we are fixers by nature, however, during this time I learned that I am not able to "fix" the episode. Therefore, I don't try fixing it because I understand how traumatic the episode is for her in the moment and I do not want to minimize what my wife is experiencing. I give her space not because I don't want to be bothered, but so that she is able to learn how to manage that episode.

I have heard some stories where the woman loses her sex drive, this could really have the husband thinking all types of negative thoughts. Although I did ask questions at the beginning of this journey, I thank God that I don't have to deal with that episode.

I believe it is critically essential to have a consistent prayer life. Having a prayer life has made it easier for me once I recognized the signs. My prayer life equipped me with the wisdom of what to say and or if I even needed to say something at all.

My strength was found in God's Word; it enabled me not to minimize my wife's feelings but instead to give encouragement. I must be honest, this journey takes patience, but the better your relationship prior to perimenopause the more equipped you will be to deal with this season of life. Having a relationship with Jesus Christ will eliminate erroneous accusations and mindsets that put you at odds with each other.

Be intentional to enjoy the days when it's good, although other episodes will come, realize those too shall pass. During the season of your wife's perimenopause journey allow this time to call to your remembrance your vows as a *covenant* and not a contract.

PEARL TO PONDER WILL BE

😍 During this journey one of the greatest gifts a man can give to his wife is unconditional love. Your unconditional love will help boost her self-esteem on those days where she does not *feel* attractive, even when you tell her how beautiful she is. Your unconditional love will encourage her to accomplish goals she thought she was incapable of handling. Your unconditional love will empower her to see herself in positives ways that she never saw herself before. Your unconditional love, commitment and dedication is a representation of your relationship with Jesus Christ and it will reaffirm her confidence in Jesus Christ. As a result, the season she is in will not only pass, but God will get all the glory because you as her husband allowed the Holy Spirit to work in and through you not only for the betterment of your wife and marriage but also as an example for someone else.

WOMAN'S SELF-PLEDGE:

I _____ understand there's no getting around this thing called perimenopause that will lead to THE BIG M (menopause). Therefore, I will need to learn more about my body, as well as to listen more intently to my body. Being aware that during The BIG M, and the transition to that point, my needs have changed. The good that can come out of this is that I can choose to give myself permission to re-prioritize my relationships and the areas of life that are causing me stress.

I _____ pledge and solemnly resolve, in the midst of the physical and emotional changes of perimenopause, to embrace this season of my life and seek God for His guidance, comfort and support through His Word and prayer. I will prayerfully resist the urge to complain during any portion of this journey but will live with a spirit of contentment (Philippians 4:11-13).

On this journey of perimenopause, some days seem dark and unpredictable. But keep in mind that like death and taxes, you can't avoid perimenopause or THE BIG M so you might as well embrace it. Once I embraced this season of my life it helped me to accept that the same Creator who gave me the ability to have children and enjoy sex with my husband also ordained this time in a woman's life.

In life you will experience many transitions, some good, some bad, some you have control over and others you won't. Life can be an emotional roller coaster. But I want to encourage you and let you in on a little secret. It is during this perimenopausal/THE BIG M season of life when many women wrote their first bestseller, went back to college, switched careers; they realized and executed their passion. All these amazing transformations may never have taken place had it not been for the biggest and most glorious change of all—perimenopause and The Big M. Now take those hot flashes and allow them to ignite something new and exciting in your life!

AHHHHH!!! I Can't Take This Anymore!

Other's Perspective of My Journey

AHHHHH!!! I Can't Take This Anymore!

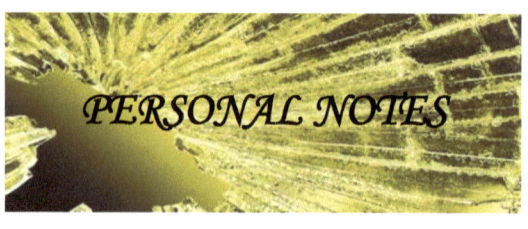

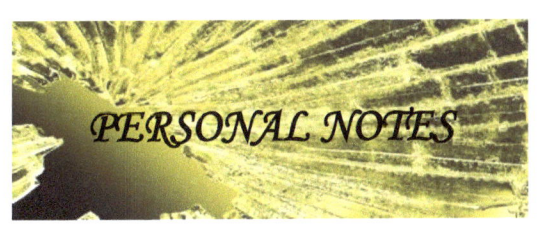

AHHHHH!!! I Can't Take This Anymore!

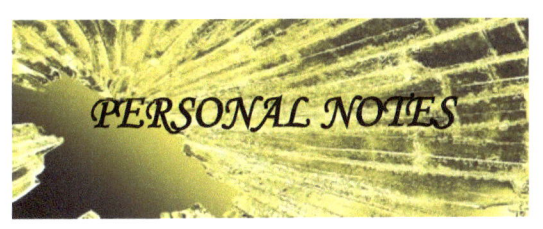

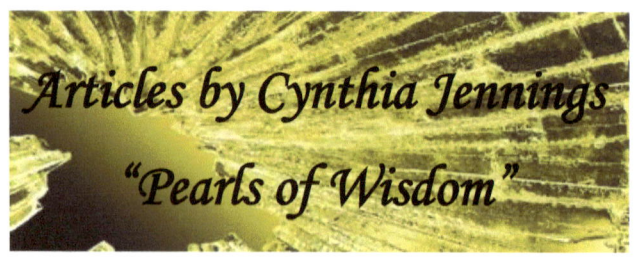

P.M.S. (Prayer, Meditation, Self-Control)

"I'm sooo hot! God, if you don't help me I'm going to lose my mind!" I know at first glance it appears that I'm talking about what all women will experience during perimenopause or menopause. Although the phrase fits, but what I'm actually talking about is the emotion of frustration that builds up when we're working in ministry, interacting with church members, on the job, and at home, dealing with our spouse and children. The unexpected, unwanted feeling of frustration rises to a boiling point. It seems like, "they just don't understand." So when we are asked to do *one more thing* before any other task has been completed it puts our stress load over the top.

As a pastor's wife, I have often said to myself, "I'm sooo hot!" As women we have all been at that point; if you don't hold on to your lid, you too will have the unexpected, unwanted experience of saying, "I'm sooo hot." When I feel myself "getting hot" I immediately stop what I'm doing and pray. Once I'm at the point of "getting hot," I have to acknowledge that I have overextended myself or mismanaged my time, causing me to become anxious.

Philippians 4:6 states, "Do not be anxious about anything, but in everything by prayer and supplication with thanksgiving let your requests be made known to God." Prayer refocuses me, putting Jesus at the forefront of my mind so I am able to renew my mind, (Philippians 2:5) and die to my flesh (2 Corinthians 4:16). Prayer allows me to intentionally think and meditate on His Word to calm the "hotness."

My favorite scripture, which I meditate on often is, Philippians 4:8-9; it reads, *"Finally, brethren, whatsoever things are true, whatsoever things are just, whatsoever things are pure, whatsoever things are lovely, whatsoever things are of good report; if there be any virtue, and if there be any praise, think on these things. Those things, which ye have both learned, and received, and heard, and seen in me, do: and the God of peace shall be with you."* *(KJV)* Dealing with the issue of "I'm sooo hot" is a matter of discipline and self-control.

I know you're probably thinking of the mindset that says, "I'm sooo hot" is warranted. That may be true, but we must remember we don't want to be a stumbling block to another sister in Christ, or a hindrance to a sister who has yet to accept Jesus Christ as her Lord and Savior. *"All things are lawful unto me, but all things are not expedient: all things are lawful for me, but I will not be brought under the power of any."* 1 Corinthians 6:12 *(KJV)*.

When I get the unexpected, unwanted feeling of "I'm sooo hot," the following three steps are essential to my cooling down process. I pray they will help you as well.

1. ***Pray:*** Ephesians 6:18; 1 Thessalonians 5:17; James 5:16

2. ***Meditate:*** Psalm 1:2; Psalm 19:14; Joshua 1:8

3. ***Use self-control:*** Proverbs 25:28; Proverbs 29:11; Ephesians 6:12; 1 Peter 4:7

The Feeling of Being Ill Equipped

As Pastor's wife, I wear many hats. Some are familiar hats that I am comfortable wearing; this makes the task easy to complete. Some are brand new hats that don't fit so well and I am reluctant to put them on. I am apprehensive about taking on the new task because I feel ill-equipped.

In the role of Pastor's wife, I am expected to "mind my P's & Q's" at all times. I am expected to say and do the right things, give great godly advice to the women in our ministry and encourage them whenever they feel ill-equipped for a task. Well, who is there to model and reciprocate those things for pastor's wives?

I often recall the words my husband said before he stepped into his calling as a founding pastor, *"It's time."* Those words produced a feeling of fear and being ill-equipped that gripped me like a glove. All I could focus on was the fact that I knew nothing about being a pastor's wife. After 13 years I sometimes get that same feeling.

When this feeling overshadows me and anxiety rises up I quote 2 Timothy 1:7, "For God hath not given us the spirit of fear; but of power, and of love, and of a sound mind."

This scripture helps to release any fear or anxiety that causes the ill-equipped feeling. This scripture also empowers me to accept the task that may cause the ill-equipped feeling.

God loves me. I know this because He gave up His only Son to die for my sins. Jesus experienced some very difficult situations for us, but in the midst of going through those difficult situations His focus was on completing the task that God had given him. With this in mind I am confident that whatever task is before me I know God loves me and He will give me the strength to complete the task. A sound mind is a disciplined mind. With God's help I can discipline my mind to focus on Him and meditate on His word. This puts my mind at peace.

When my mind is at peace I no longer view the task from my flesh and inabilities, but through the eyes of God. I trust that He will give me the wisdom and the ability to complete the task, relieving me of the pressure and anxiety of feeling ill equipped.

As a Pastor's wife this ill-equipped feeling surfaces more than I would like to admit. When it does I immediately stop trusting in my own abilities and trust in

God's ability.

"Trust in the L<small>ORD</small> with all thine heart; and lean not unto thine own understanding. In all thy ways acknowledge him, and he shall direct thy paths." (Proverbs 3:5-6, KJV).

A new hat has been given to me. So I'm taking a deep breath and I am loudly quoting Proverbs 3:5-6 and 2 Timothy 1:7.

The Blessing of UNGLUEDNESS

As women there are challenging situations in life that can cause us to feel like we are becoming UNGLUED. During a season of UNGLUEDNESS the enemy dominates the mind with all the things you need to do, how to execute getting it all done, using demeaning and intimidating words like, "that's too hard, you won't be able to do it." When I go into prayer in this UNGLUED state I oftentimes go before God incognito (or so I think) hoping God doesn't recognize me (my heart). In other words, I went before God being deceptive about my feelings, having doubt in my heart, and pretending everything is okay.

When in a state of UNGLUEDNESS I also pray fashionably before God. Fancy empty words just to say I prayed, but not being genuinely transparent before God (as if God didn't know my heart and what was really going on). Unrecognized UNGLUDENSS will lead to shadiness because you don't want anyone to see how UNGLUED you are. When you become shady your life becomes spiritually dark, chaotic and discombobulated. But the **recognition** of being UNGLUED is a blessing because at that moment I understood and remembered that I am not in control.

Regardless of the depth of the UNGLUEDNESS, when I hear that still, small voice telling me that I'm UNGLUED, I make a conscious choice to stop and refocus on God's Word. I trust the guidance of the Holy Spirit who gives instruction on how to thrive and have peace in a season of UNGLUEDNESS. Because I understand that this may be God's way of getting my attention to work out of me what He needs to get out of me for His purpose and glory.

I am so grateful that God allowed me to stop and refocus on His Word to guide me in the midst of UNGLUEDENSS. Now the enemy doesn't have room to dominate in that area, if I ever become UNGLUED again. You too have the power to thrive in a season of UNGLUEDNESS!

"Peace I leave with you, my peace I give unto you: not as the world giveth, give I unto you. Let not your heart be troubled, neither let it be afraid" (John 14:27, KJV) "For God is not the author of confusion, but of peace, as in all churches of the saints." (1 Corinthians 14:33, KJV)

Royal Candlelight Christian Publishing Company

PRESENTS

*Author
Cynthia Jennings*

BIOGRAPHY: The First Lady and Ministry Director of Total Christian Life Ministry of Joliet, IL, Cynthia Jennings faithfully serves under the leadership of her husband, Founder and Pastor Tracy Jennings.

First Lady Jennings has been successful at the non-profit level as a former Director for The Salvation Army's Head Start program where she prepared her site from beginning to completion for accreditation. She was a partner in a real estate appraisal company. As well as being heavily involved in the community by serving on several boards and filled the role of Vice President for the School Parent Teacher Organization.

As one of the founding members, First Lady Jennings has been able to use her organizational and administrative skills acquired while working at the non-profit level to help build Total Christian Life Ministry from its inception. She compiled and completed all state and federal documents from the assumed name to the 501(c)3 registering as a non-profit organization recognized by the State of Illinois. She has also been able to assist other start-up ministries with the process of compiling and completing state and federal documents.

First Lady Jennings has been instrumental in creating church by-laws, auxiliary job descriptions, biblical assessments for ministry leaders, locating vendors, as well as maintaining and keeping all important and legal documents current. She is also the overseer of several auxiliaries. She has a passion for ministry, but her greatest passion is to see women living at their fullest God-given potential. On May 27, 2010 she heard the call, and **PEARLS** Women's ministry was birthed. Through this ministry First Lady Jennings helps women identify, own, accept, and obtain deliverance from their hurts. The process is "dirty," but the purpose is to get women to a place in Christ where they see themselves as Christ sees them, fearfully and wonderfully made (Psalms 139:14). On November 2, 2016, the Lord also placed a prayer burden in First Lady Jennings concerning Pastor's Wives and Ministry Mates, (the wives of ministry leaders). As a result, **Empowerment Place: You're Not Alone** (EPYNA) was birthed. EPYNA's purpose is to create synergy between Pastors Wives and Ministry Mates to develop a community where we support and encourage, as well as give and receive words of wisdom to help us manage times when we feel as if we are all alone (1 Corinthians 12: 8-10).

First Lady Jennings holds a Bachelor of Arts in Early Childhood Education from the University of Iowa; she received training in Spiritual Formation and Discipleship from Moody Theological Seminary, and has been awarded her Master of Arts in Christian Life Coaching and Mentorship from Trinity Theological Seminary.

Her greatest blessing is being married to her husband, the anointed Pastor Tracy Jennings, and having the honor of being the mother to two amazing adult children, Reggie and Traci.

Royal Candlelight Christian Publishing Company

"Royalty in the Making"

Share Your Thoughts with This Author

We want to hear from you about this amazing book. Please go on Amazon.com and leave a rating and a comment to show this author how much you enjoyed her ***JOURNEY!***

CHRISTIAN AUTHORS INTERESTED IN PUBLISHING

WITH

ROYAL CANDLELIGHT CHRISTIAN PUBLISHING COMPANY

check out our website, email us, or give us a call

(909) 999-2433

e-mail us at: www.royalcandlelight.com or royal.candlelight@hotmail.com

And be blessed!

www.ingramcontent.com/pod-product-compliance
Lightning Source LLC
Chambersburg PA
CBHW042304150426
43197CB00001B/12